MODERN ICONS

BOB MARLEY

Acknowledgments

With very grateful thanks to Philip Dodd, Lucinda Hawksley,
Helen Johnson, Morse Modaberi and to John Stickland,
Gary Stickland and the staff of the National Sound Archive
for their help in the research of this book.

Scotty Bennett is an experienced music journalist, who has
written for *Echoes* magazine – as well as for other publications
– for the past twenty years, concentrating on reggae. In that
time he has interviewed most of the major names in reggae,
including the late Bob Marley and Peter Tosh.

Modern Icons conceived and developed
for and with Virgin Publishing Ltd by Flame Tree Publishing,
a part of The Foundry Creative Media Company Limited,
The Long House, Antrobus Road, Chiswick, London W4 5HY.

ISBN 0-312-17937-5

Library of Congress Cataloging-in-Publication Data available on request

First published in the United Kingdom in 1997 by Virgin Publishing Ltd.

First U.S. edition

10 9 8 7 6 5 4 3 2 1

MODERN ICONS

BOB MARLEY

Introduction by Scotty Bennett

St. Martin's Press
New York

CONTENTS

CONTENTS

INTRODUCTION

O n 11 May 1981 the Hon. Robert Nesta Marley OM died of cancer at the Cedars Of Lebanon hospital in Miami, aged 36. His body was flown back to his Jamaican birthplace where he was given a state funeral. The day before the burial, in excess of 40,000 mourners filed past his coffin as it lay in state in the National Arena, draped with the black, gold and green Jamaican flag.

During his brief life, Marley had emerged from the slums of Kingston's Trenchtown district to achieve worldwide fame. He was the first Third World superstar and his music addressed the problems and aspirations of its people, indeed of all mankind. Just a few weeks prior to his death, the Jamaican government under new Prime Minister Edward Seaga awarded the island's most famous son the Jamaican Order of Merit. The year before, Marley's crowning moment had come when he played a concert in Salisbury to celebrate the independence of the new nation of Zimbabwe. It was a fitting tribute to a man whose songs like 'Revolution', 'War' and 'Zimbabwe' itself had helped hasten the end of the Rhodesian regime during its final desperate days.

In the years since his death, the man's stature has increased in currency with every passing season. At the time of writing, his posthumous album 'Legend' has sold in excess of ten million copies since its release in 1984, while the extensive four-CD, 78 track 'Songs

Of Freedom' anthology, issued in 1992, has shifted two million units. His image has become one of the most keenly recognised in the whole world and his role as a figurehead for the oppressed and underclass in each of the five continents is synonymous in the Nineties with that of Che Guevara during the Sixties.

Bob Marley grew up in the heart of Kingston's maelstrom. His Second Street home in Trenchtown bordered on rival districts Denham Town, Jones Town and Greenwich Town. Across the other side of the Spanish Town Road, behind the cemetery, stood the infamous Dungle area, a squatters' encampment of improvised tin shelters and shacks, populated by wild Rastas and their breed, and scavengers of all types.

The teenage Marley was shaped by his past and present environment. He was a racially mixed country boy who had come to live in the big city, and he was determined to hold his own and be as rude as any of the local rude boys. His prowess as a fighter earned him the nickname Tuff Gong.

He had gone to live in Kingston in 1957, rejoining his mother who had moved

to the city two years earlier. Here they shared a yard with the extended family of carpenter Thaddeus Livingston, whose eldest son Bunny soon became Bob's close friend and singing partner. As youths, the pair would frequent the informal harmony lessons held just around the corner in the Third Street yard of singer Joe Higgs. There the pair met up for the first time with another Higgs aspirant, a lanky lad named Peter Tosh, and under the elder man's guidance, the three teenagers soon began wailing in unison.

Marley made contact with local record label proprietor Leslie Kong and the outcome was a recording session, duly followed by a couple of releases ascribed to Robert Marley – 'Judge Not' and 'One Cup Of Coffee' (Marley reportedly received £20 for the session) – but nothing further ensued, since neither tune sold. Marley resumed singing with Bunny and Peter, adding another youth named Junior Braithwaite and a girl called Beverley Kelso to the line-up. Now operating as a vocal quintet, they had a name for themselves too: The Wailers.

By the end of the following year, Higgs decided the group were sufficiently rehearsed and introduced them to one of the island's leading record producers, Clement Dodd, who ran the Studio One record label. Impressed by the Bob and Bunny composition 'Simmer Down', a brisk ska, he booked a session and released it in time for Christmas. By the end of January 1964, it was the top tune on the local chart.

The appeal of 'Simmer Down' was that the song caught the spirit of and addressed itself directly to the emergent rude boy cult, then growing daily more visible on the streets of western Kingston. Its adherents were the young ghetto dispossessed, angry and violent and increasingly armed with ratchets, and even guns and home-made bombs, victims of poverty and politics, but also of a generation gap that was causing confrontation between youth and authority simultaneously in Europe and the US.

In due course, The Wailers would record a number of titles on the same topic for Studio One, paeans to the rudies such as 'Put It On', 'Rude Boy', 'Good Good Rudie', 'Let Him Go (Rude Boy Get Bail)' and

'I Stand Predominate'. For the present however, Dodd preferred to groom the group on the US soul model, and their follow-up 'It Hurts To Be Alone', was a frail ballad written and sung by Junior Braithwaite.

By the following year, Bob Marley was working at the studio day and night, and even sleeping there, Dodd having given him a room at the back after his mother had emigrated to Delaware in search of better paid work. At the end of 1965, Beverley Kelso left and Braithwaite quit to live in the States, leaving the trio of Bob, Bunny and Peter, with additional harmonies supplemented by whoever happened to be around the studio at the time.

One such was Rita Anderson, who otherwise sung with another Studio One act The Soulettes, a female vocal trio. In time she and Bob began courting and soon a child was due. In February 1966, a few days after his 21st birthday and the day after his marriage to Rita, Bob Marley kissed his bride and their daughter Ciddy goodbye and boarded a plane to join his mother in Delaware. He stayed in the States for only nine months and on his return gathered the group together again for one final Studio One session and

another hit with 'Bend Down Low'. This was before disputes over royalties and differences of opinion on musical policy led to a parting of the ways with Dodd, and their setting up of an independent label Wail'M'Soul'M, a brave act for a ghetto group in Jamaica with no uptown connections. A dozen or so sides emerged on the label during 1967-68, but lack of distribution and exposure meant limited returns and when Bunny was jailed for possession of ganja the venture was abandoned.

Meanwhile, the American singer Johnny Nash had recently settled in Jamaica and recorded a string of international hits utilising a pronounced Jamaican rock-steady beat. In time, he ran into Bob and Rita Marley and on hearing some of the Gong's lyrics, invited Bob and his wife to his home in the smart Kingston suburbs. As a result, the American hired Bob and the other two Wailers as songwriters and in early 1969, following Bunny's release from prison, The Wailers began laying demo recordings of their songs for Nash's Cayman Music publishing company. Later that same year, they also joined forces with the brilliant but erratic record producer Lee Perry for a collaboration that was to mark a major change in the group's development – some thirty sides laid over the next couple of years witnessed the creation of their most powerful and imaginative work to date.

In late 1971, Bob and the rest of The Wailers flew to London, where Johnny Nash's manager Danny Sims was trying to set up a deal for them with his artist's label CBS. At the time, Nash's latest LP, 'I Can See Clearly Now', was a best-seller all over the world, and Bob had written four of the album's tracks. Sims was convinced that The Wailers too were poised for the big breakthrough, but in the event their sole release for CBS, a new Bob Marley tune 'Reggae On Broadway', did nothing at all and CBS lost interest. Then Nash and Sims flew out to the States on business, leaving The Wailers penniless and stranded, without even their return fare to Jamaica. It was at this point that Bob Marley walked into the offices of Island Records and demanded an interview with the label's Jamaican owner Chris Blackwell.

Blackwell had recognised early the commercial potential of Jamaican music beyond its indigenous audience when his production of Millie Small's 'My Boy Lollipop' became the first UK ska hit in 1964, and he was convinced that with proper exposure a good reggae act might achieve results similar to his rock artists. He'd toyed with signing the better known Maytals for their singer Toots's flamboyant, Baptist-derived vocal style but naught came of it. The Wailers held an underground reputation from the rude boy era, and their militant rebel stance had lately attracted the notice of those involved in the black political scene too, so when Bob Marley walked into the offices of Island Records, he and Blackwell were ready for each other. The upshot was the group's plane fare back to Jamaica and an advance on their new LP.

Though the group's debut album for Island 'Catch A Fire' sold only steadily on its release in early 1973, it did alert the interest of the rock media, which until now had regarded reggae as noise fit only for cretinous skinheads. The Wailers visited Europe and the US that summer for a short promotional tour, and at the end of the year their follow-up 'Burnin'' was released. One of the songs on the new set was 'I Shot The Sheriff', which became an international hit when covered by Eric Clapton. Suddenly, Bob Marley was big news.

Sadly, Bob, Bunny and Peter began drifting apart. Bunny Wailer wanted a peaceful life in the Jamaican hills and positively refused to tour with the group. Peter Tosh was resentful at what he perceived as Island's emphasis on Marley's leading role, at the expense of himself and Bunny. Their departure completed The Wailers's transformation from a singing trio into a roots rock reggae band called Bob Marley And The Wailers. For the 'Natty Dread' album in 1975, Bob Marley now occupied centre stage, backed by a band of top-flight Jamaican musicians. He recruited his wife Rita and two of the island's leading lady singers Marcia Griffiths and Judy Mowatt as The I-Three providing harmony support. The outfit toured Europe and the US to ecstatic reception where, following a wild show at London's Lyceum Theatre, a live recording of 'No Woman, No Cry' was released to give Marley his first UK hit.

Back in Jamaica in 1976, the group laid tracks for a new LP 'Rastaman Vibrations', amid the turmoil of an election year. By this time, The Wailers and entourage were living in a mansion in uptown

Kingston given to Marley by Blackwell, and towards the year's end the singer agreed to play a concert in Kingston's National Heroes Park – an event seen locally as a political platform for the ruling People's National Party of Prime Minister Michael Manley. Two days prior to the appointed show, a gang of gunmen burst into the Hope Road house, weapons blazing. In their wake, both Bob and Rita were shot, as were a couple of Marley's friends, while his manager Don Taylor lay sprawled near to death in a pool of his own blood. Fortunately, no one was killed and Marley was persuaded that the concert should go ahead as planned. The morning after the show, he left Jamaica.

During his exile in the UK in 1977, tracks were laid in Island's London studios for his subsequent two LPs, 'Exodus' and 'Kaya'. During a European tour that summer he sustained an injury to his foot which would not heal. His doctor detected cancer cells and advised the amputation of his big toe. This Marley declined.

It was more than a year after the shooting incident that he returned to Jamaica, to play the One Love concert in Kingston's National Stadium in April 1978. Ever since the Caribbean island had gained independence from Britain in 1962, the opposing People's National Party and Jamaican Labour Party had engaged in open feuding. Much of the ghetto fratricide was perpetuated by gangs of thugs hired by the political parties to foment unrest in rival constituencies. Now a truce had been declared and Bob Marley was cast as its ambassador, his safety guaranteed by both sides. The event was attended by the political elite of Jamaica and was a moment of supreme honour in Marley's career. During his performance, Marley contrived to clasp the arm of Prime Minister Michael Manley together with that of the Leader of the Opposition Edward Seaga in a three-fisted salute, as the two politicians smiled frozenly in obvious distaste.

After an arduous world tour to promote 'Kaya', work began on a new LP, 'Survival'. Espousing Marley's embrace of the wider black struggle on songs like 'So Much Trouble In The World', 'Africa Unite', 'Zimbabwe' and the title track, it was his most militant album of all – and on its release in autumn 1979 the song 'Zimbabwe' swiftly became a rallying cry throughout Africa. Following their reception at the Independence ceremony for the new nation of Zimbabwe in May 1980, the group set out on another tour to promote their next LP. In September, they began the US leg of the tour, but within a week it had been cancelled following Marley's collapse while jogging in New York's Central Park. The official explanation was exhaustion, but privately doctors confirmed that cancer tissue had been detected

throughout the singer's body and he was given mere weeks to live. He was taken to a specialist cancer clinic in Germany where skilful attention ensured his survival for a further six months, but when the end was finally in sight, Marley was flown back to Miami and died there days later.

Bob Marley's death signalled the end of an era in reggae music. Prime Minister Michael Manley's socialist experiment had foundered and, as the singer had lain dying in the clinic in Bavaria the previous year, Edward Seaga's JLP were returned to power on the island for the first time in eight years. A change in government in a country like Jamaica created a climactic shift in power. The Rasta rhetoric which had dominated reggae throughout the previous decade disappeared from the music and a fresh breed of singers and producers from the JLP territories began to make their mark.

This was the era of the dancehall style, when the music returned to its roots in the sound systems and again began addressing itself. Played live, in concert halls and stadiums, the roots rock reggae derivation of the music had won it audiences all over the world, but this is not where its true heart lay. Suddenly, live reggae began to look passé by the side of a new generation of sweet singers and fast talkers dealing with the perennial ghetto preoccupations of love and lust, good times, gold chains and guns. Like elsewhere in the world, the Eighties had arrived in Jamaica.

Ignorant of the political and social ramifications and alienated by the dancehall genre's ritual and self-reference, the rock media quickly grew disillusioned with reggae. There was much discussion of the music having lost its way and needing a new leader in place of Bob, much like the futile search for a new Beatles ten years earlier.

In truth, Bob Marley had little effect on reggae's development back then or since. The music's real pioneers were the producers like

Clement Dodd, Duke Reid and Lee Perry. The prodigal keyboards player Jackie Mittoo, who also died of cancer in December 1990, built many of the Studio One rhythms that have had the most apparent influence on the music's subsequent development in the dancehall and ragga modes. In the sound system dances, people prefer their music either sweet and sentimental or else rough and ready and Bob Marley's later work satisfied neither requirements. From his moment of international fame in the mid-Seventies, the music of Bob Marley And The Wailers was no longer played by the reggae sound systems.

Marley's lasting contribution was something other than this. All the contradictions of Jamaican society were inherent in his mixed blood and by bringing his experience of this to bear on his music, the singer gave reggae to a worldwide audience. And all he ever had were songs of freedom, redemption songs . . . .

SCOTTY BENNETT

VOICE OF THE GHETTO

In December 1976, seven armed men attacked Bob Marley's house on Hope Road in Kingston. In the ensuing shooting, Marley, his wife Rita, his manager Don Taylor, and a family friend were all injured, the latter two seriously. Thankfully all survived, but Marley and Rita left their Jamaican home for eighteen months. This was the first recorded assassination attempt on a major music star, four years before John Lennon was felled by Mark Chapman. But this was not the act of a deluded stalker, this was politically driven. Marley had publicly given his support to Michael Manley, the Prime Minister of Jamaica, who was then involved in a bitter election campaign. This was proof that for Marley, his music and his lifestyle were inextricably linked with the island of his birth. He could not avoid delivering a message in that music. And once he had embraced Rastafarianism in the late Sixties and early Seventies, he was destined to broadcast the message of his religion, along with all its apparently paradoxical conflicts (paradoxical to the outsider): the militancy of black pride and the message of universal love, the revolution and revelation, the spirituality and the aggression born out of anger. Rarely has one musician been the recipient of such a responsibility – by the time of his death from cancer in 1981, Marley had become the voice of black awareness, the figurehead of the Rastafarian movement, and an ambassador for reggae music whose

talents thrust its rhythms into the consciousness of the rest of the world. His global superstardom sprung directly out of the environment he had grown up in, and his experiences of poverty and hardship in Trenchtown, where he met fellow Wailers Bunny Livingston and Peter Tosh, and where the music that he took far beyond the shores of the island of Jamaica had been created, cultivated and charged with the destiny of its people.

Who's a rock star? I'm not a rock star. I'm a Rastaman defending repatriation for black people to go home to Africa and peace on earth for all mankind.

Bob Marley

Rastafarianism is a complex set of beliefs that found a resonance in pockets of the Jamaican people. The growth of its following there had been fuelled by a visit to the island in 1966 by Ethiopia's Emperor Haile Selassie, the religion's chosen spiritual leader. Rita Marley had first turned to Rastafarianism following Selassie's visit, and in turn Bob Marley began to absorb its beliefs, and from there adopt the lifestyle. This was no once a week socially acceptable form of religion, it was a commitment that diffused into every action, every thought and every utterance. From his lyrics, to press interviews, to touring decisions, all now were permeated by Marley's deeply held convictions.

The white man has nothing he can give us, you know – only death. That's why I & I is Rasta because we know death has nothing against I & I.

Bob Marley, *Melody Maker*, 1979

What was once Rasta culture is now Jamaican culture.
There's no dividing the two.

Perry Hazell, producer of the film *The Harder They Come*, NME, 1975

You change if you change from Babylon to Rasta, but you
can't change from Rasta to anything. When the truth
awaken in you you can't do anything but accept the truth.

Bob Marley, 1978

Bob Marley, Wailer frontman, spokesman, alarming singer of
equally alarming songs, is the Bob Dylan of reggae. He is cosmic
mutant, sci-fi materialisation of some futurist human being – wild and
angry young man with tribulations on his mind. He has the Peace of
Ras Tafari. The obsessions of his lyrics – Fire, Perfect Love, Revolution
To Come – are flowers rammed lovingly down the gun barrels of
authority, bombs placed lovingly in its pockets. He is fly on the plastic
wallpapers of Caribbean Society, exorcist for his people. He's been
inside and outside the government yards and he shot the sheriff.

Idris Walters, *Let It Rock*, 1974

Being good Rastafarians, the Wailers believe that everything is
pre-ordained by Jah, and that the cold weather was a sign that
they had displeased Jah, and that He didn't want them to play here.

Island press officer, December 1973, after The Wailers
cancelled ten dates because of the UK's wintry conditions

Through Marley the specific Rastafarian message of freedom, of a return to a spiritual homeland found a response worldwide – as a touchstone for any disaffected group, fighting against oppression, real or perceived. And in Jamaica itself he became a focus for political activism. Before Live Aid and its successors tried to remove the rock industry's guilt at its own hedonistic self-absorption, Marley had been trying to use the power of music to influence politics: at the One Love Peace concert of 1978 he had brought together for one brief moment the island's bitter political rivals Michael Manley and Edward Seaga.

Bob Marley is our Che. Good God! Somebody even tried to assassinate him. The sanitized, consumer-centred, inferiority-complex-motivated white Western (and mainly student) audience need a focal point, a comfortable pinpoint, an envelope . . . Marley is now an entertainer, a poster, an institution, the rebel, the image all these young people need.
Ian Penman, *NME*, 1978

I said that peace will take many years, but I'm willing to give it a chance today.
Bob Marley, at the One Love Peace concert, 1978

When Little Richard stood up at his piano and hollered Tutti Frutti, he sounded like a man who'd just broken out of prison. Otis Redding, Jimi Hendrix and even Bruce Springsteen have since reached similar moments of sudden and usually sexual electricity, but only Bob Marley has ever built a major body of work in which virtually every song is shot through with an ever dawning sense of freedom.

Mark Cooper, Q magazine, 1992

My music fights against the system that teaches to live and die.

Bob Marley, 1976

Jamaica was the heartland of Marley's music, and music was Jamaica's lifeblood: by 1976 there were some 75 independent record producers and 15 recording studios on the island, although reggae continued to be seen as ghetto music. Marley never abandoned his roots or Jamaica despite his success, taking over the house on Hope Road that was owned by Chris Blackwell, head of Island Records, ignoring the envious comments of former Trenchtown acquaintances, and continuing to observe the Rasta lifestyle.

You look into my yard. It's a ghetto. This is ghetto you're looking at. Look out there. I've just brought the ghetto uptown.
Bob Marley, *Melody Maker*, 1979

If you are a black Jamaican and you come from Trenchtown, or your friends come from Trenchtown, and you are writing your own songs and producing reggae music, the natural source of your music is your environment.
Chris Blackwell, *Melody Maker*, 1976

When you smoke herb, herb reveal yourself to you. All the wickedness you do, the herb reveal it all to yourself – your conscience. Show up yourself clear. Is only a natural t'ing, and it grow like the tree.
Bob Marley, *Rolling Stone*, 1975

T'ing is . . . you shouldn't smoke too much. You shouldn't smoke 'erb like me.
Bob Marley, *NME*, 1978

WAILIN'

· ·

*Bob Marley met Bunny 'Wailer' Livingston when they lived in the
same yard in Trenchtown – and their relationship was strengthened
when Marley's mother Cedella and Livingston's father Thaddeus had
a daughter, Alice, in 1962. Both teenagers were by then involved in
the music scene, absorbing its distinctive flavour. Local musicians had
long adapted the music of other cultures, whether the swing band
sound of the Forties, or bebop and R&B in the Fifties, but their sense
of national identity had been reinforced as Jamaica anticipated
independence from British colonial rule (it finally arrived in August
1962). The official broadcasting station in Jamaica was a Caribbean
version of the BBC, so for fresh musical input the few people who
owned radios tuned into the American stations broadcasting out of
Florida. To bring that music to a wider audience, mobile sound
systems were constructed. On turntables in converted vans, much
sought-after records acquired on trips to the US were played to
audiences by the likes of Sir Coxsone Dodd or Duke Reid. In due
course the best sound systems decided they needed more material
and created the means to record and release their own sounds. Bob
and Bunny benefited from this spirit of enterprise, initially learning
and honing their vocal skills with Joe Higgs, a local musician who
organised musical sessions at his Trenchtown home (where the two
met another young musician, Peter Tosh) and studying rhythm with*

drummer Alvin 'Seeco' Patterson. Marley, Livingston and Tosh – initially joined by Junior Braithwaite and Beverley Kelso – began recording their distinctive harmonies in 1963, scoring an immediate hit with the Marley composition 'Simmer Down'. The Wailin' Wailers, as they called themselves, were regulars on the Jamaican charts, and carved out their own niche in 1966 by releasing 'Rude Boy', which linked them to the hardheads of the Trenchtown area and gave them a tougher image. A series of ups and downs followed, but by the time they signed to Island Records in 1972 and provided a fresh blast of excitement for the rest of the world, they had already paid their dues and learnt their craft in a decade of solid and invaluable experience.

People forget that they'd been together for ten years. You had had three giants within one band, all with different ideas. Suddenly they were thrown into the limelight and they needed a face, and that face was always going to be Marley.

Photographer **Dennis Morris**, *Mojo*, 1995

In 1966, there was a hiatus in the career of The Wailers. Marley left Jamaica for a nine-month spell in America, where he built up savings working in a factory in Delaware. On his return he and wife Rita set up a local record store and then launched a short-lived record label, Wail'M'Soul'M. It was the involvement of producer Lee 'Scratch' Perry which got the reunited Wailers back on track, improving and exploring their potential.

Despite the massive international success and impact achieved by Bob Marley during his sojourn with Island Records, your actual serious connoisseurs maintain that the real classic Wailers sides were those cut with master-producer Lee Perry a few years earlier, when the rock-steady era was beginning to yield to the new reggae beat and the original trio of Marley, Peter Tosh and Bunny Wailer were at the height of their collective powers.

Charles Shaar Murray, *Q* magazine, 1987

Anything can happen in music, we only experiment. It's never wise to limit yourself. Them people think that I should do the same this year as last! Maybe them people don't like it, but new people like it. You can't stay in one place.

Bob Marley, 1974

As far as I'm concerned every song that Bob Marley sing is good. That is the only artist in Jamaica that I really admire and nothing Bob can do can be wrong as far as I'm concerned.

Lee Perry, *Black Music*, 1975

Just when The Wailers were at the point of breakthrough, Tosh and Livingston left, leading to conjecture that Island Records's emphasis on Marley, sidelining the contributions of the other two, finally broke up the trio that had stuck together for so long. Other theories were that Tosh was too volatile, too brilliant, and not prepared to play the music industry game, or that Bunny Livingston didn't want to leave Jamaica and take the music to an international audience. Whatever the reasons, their departure left the field clear for Marley to become the recognisable face of reggae.

Mebbe they don' like tour too much, but they're still me brethren so . . . greeyat, y'know, we still play together sometime. But music is music and me miss the music if the music leave – but the music stay . . . .
Bob Marley, *NME*, 1975

I left, and I imagine Peter will tell you the same, because I saw the tree differently – Bob saw it one way and I saw it another. But we're all seeing the same tree. All Rasta!
Bunny Wailer, *Melody Maker*, 1976

I feel Peter Tosh was want to have adventures himself, him talented enough and mebbe him want something better than this.
Bob Marley, *Melody Maker*, 1975

With the break-up of the original
Wailers, Marley's musical options
widened. Vocal harmonies were
provided by the I-Threes – Rita
Marley, Judy Mowatt and Marcia
Griffiths, three of the finest female
vocalists out of Jamaica – adding
an extra element of sensuality.
And behind additional guitarists
and keyboards, the rhythm
section of the Barrett brothers,
Carlton on drums, Aston 'Family
Man' on bass – introduced to The
Wailers in the late Sixties by Lee
Perry – exerted an ever more
powerful influence.

The Wailers' music is simultaneously a genuine *folk* music, and as technically and lyrically sophisticated, despite its superficial simplicity, as most of the produce of their contemporaries, which qualities combine to give it both its intoxicating spirituality and its riveting funk.

Charles Shaar Murray, *NME*, 1975

The Wailers make a psychic rainstorm of a music. It ties knots in the intestines, lacerates clots in the brain and greases a whole new set of muscles.

Idris Walters, *Let it Rock*, 1974

Bass figures that lope and stalk and aren't afraid to leave gaps. His nimble runs contrast with an almost studiedly indolent stance. Carlton Barrett is almost equally inscrutable beneath the long shadow of his hunting cap. He provides an unflagging metric for the rest of the group, going round his tomtom at most twenty times per night, paradiddles extra.

Neil Spencer, *NME*, 1975, on the Barrett brothers

Family Man Barrett doesn't toy with the bass riff, he thunders it into a convenient hole between brother Carlton's rim shot outbursts. That bass riff on 'Lively Up Yourself' claws like a magnet and sucks you out of your seat. Absolutely irresistible.

Steve Lake, *Melody Maker*, 1975

SPREADING THE WORD

* *

In 1973, the year that Island Records released The Wailers's 'Catch A Fire', the conditions were ready for their brand of reggae to make its mark on the international music scene. Their message was strong, intense and based on deep beliefs. Rock music had rarely offered any genuinely revolutionary or political pronouncements; teenage rebellion was the most it stirred up, and the message of the Summer of Love was hardly militant. Only a handful of folk-based singers could attempt the same mix of conviction and music. A fiercely committed singer – blessed with an ear for infectious melodies and rhythms – was a novelty in both the UK and the US. That Marley's message was complicated and seemingly Byzantine was not an obstacle. Although journalists frequently tied themselves up into knots trying to untangle the stream of statements and ideas that would burst forth from Marley, they weren't the target audience. The message of Rastafarianism was not aimed at a white audience, however sympathetic. But the tone of the message, its looser vibes of freedom and universal love, could easily be responded to. Another element in The Wailers's breakthrough was the role of Island Records. Its founder, Chris Blackwell, was a genuine admirer, a white Jamaican who had been distributing Jamaican records, including Marley's very first singles, since setting up the company in 1962, but he had been concentrating on rock in order to build the profile of

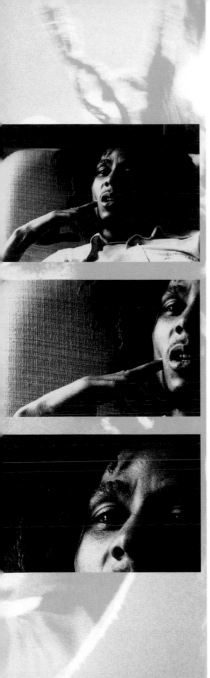

Island. When Marley and The Wailers pitched up in his London office, down on their luck after a disappointing experience with their last managers, the timing was perfect. Island had the belief, the clout, the cash, and the promotional and production know-how, to push the band hard. And the wider audience was in a receptive mood, or at least ready to be told they were in a receptive mood.

These songs, people understand them or they cyann understand them, but y'ave fe sing them just the same.
Bob Marley, 1976

There was no doubting the danceability of the reggae groove, but Marley always insisted that the words of his songs were a vital part of his music. He was not writing them to be ignored, even though he understood that commercial success, which could bring that message to a wider audience, meant that many, if not most, of his listeners might not ever truly hear what he was trying to say.

Sometime I can dig music, I can dig instrumental music. But lyrics important.
Bob Marley, *Melody Maker,* 1975

Me have to laugh sometimes when dem scribes seh me like Mick Jagger or some superstar like that. Dem have to listen close to the music, 'cos the message not the same.
Bob Marley, *Rolling Stone,* 1976

Marley is an angry young man with a mission, and that mission is to spread the creed of the Rastafari to a Western world that to him seems obsessed with triviality. Not that the doctrines here in any way lessen the enjoyment of the loping reggae rhythms, and those uniquely subtle harmonies. And that's really the beauty of the Wailers – your appreciation can go just as deep as you want.
Steve Lake, *Melody Maker,* 1973

The system want pure love songs, like ol' Frank Sinatra, they don't want not'ing with no protest, it make too much trouble.
Bob Marley, *Melody Maker,* 1978

The commercial potential of reggae sprouted simultaneously in the States and the UK. In the US, its cult status amongst black and white Americans was shattered when Eric Clapton's 1974 Number 1 hit with Marley's 'I Shot The Sheriff' made reggae hip for the whites. In the UK, where an expatriate immigrant black Caribbean community was already strong, a growing white audience was joined by young blacks rediscovering their roots. Marley was developing into a folk hero – but he was also selling records.

Marley plays to the hilt a dual spokesman for the Third World's disadvantaged and avatar of a highly commercial brand of popular music, and on 'Rastaman Vibrations' he is playing both . . . with consummate skill.

Robert Palmer, *Rolling Stone*, 1976, on 'Rastaman Vibrations'

The Wailers was the best vocal group and I group was the best little backing band at the time. So we say, Why don't we just come together and smash the world?

Aston 'Family Man' Barrett, *Mojo*, 1995

Here the monumental heaviness and primal drive of live reggae is committed to record for, to all intents and purposes, the first time. Folks who only hear the 'top' end of this music – vocals, snare and hi-hat, skanking rhythm guitar – will be culture-shocked into concussion by the true picture.

Ian MacDonald, *NME*, 1975, on 'No Woman, No Cry'

The music broke new ground in terms of sound. It was a more metropolitan kind of reggae sound. It didn't matter whether you were living in Johannesburg or Jerusalem, you could identify with that sound.

Linton Kwesi Johnson, *Mojo*, 1995

When The Wailers signed to Island in 1973 it was an unprecedented move for a rock label. The company of Traffic, Free and Jethro Tull, by then the leading independent record company in the UK, could never have done so if Chris Blackwell hadn't long championed the music of his native Jamaica. The money he provided gave Marley and his band the security, the stability and the studio time to write and work with confidence, and supplied the necessary resources of promotional, packaging and production know-how.

Bob came into the office at the right time, when there was this idea in my head that a rebel-type character could really emerge. I was dealing with rock music, which was really rebel music. I felt that would really be the way to break Jamaican music. But you needed somebody who could be that image. When Bob walked in, he really *was* that image.

Chris Blackwell, *Mojo*, 1995

Being half-caste may have troubled Marley. It certainly gave him the edge and perspective on things he needed. It's a bit like being bilingual. Tosh and Bunny were intelligent men, but they weren't able to deal with, say, Chris Blackwell in the way Marley could.

Richard Williams, Island A&R, *Mojo*, 1995

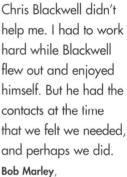

Chris Blackwell didn't help me. I had to work hard while Blackwell flew out and enjoyed himself. But he had the contacts at the time that we felt we needed, and perhaps we did.

Bob Marley,
Melody Maker, 1979

I like to think Bob Marley came to us and stayed with us because he and his band could see we loved their music, believed in them, and, most importantly, would stay with them.

Chris Blackwell,
Melody Maker, 1976

ROBERT NESTA MARLEY

* *

*The biggest black roots superstar of the Seventies was the son of a
white father and a black mother. From the day of his birth there
were tensions and conflicts at the heart of his personality. Captain
Norval Sinclair Marley was an ex-Army Crown Lands overseer
when he got Cedella Booker, a teenager in a rural village, pregnant.
They married, but Marley senior left immediately, disappearing back
to Kingston – from then until his death in 1955 his contact with
Cedella and her son would be rare. For the first years of Bob's life he
grew up in the country – he once said that he was 'a planter by
heart', but then he and his mother moved to Trenchtown where
Marley's mixed race caused him problems. There he was taunted for
being a tainted white boy. But he overcame the abuse, using his
words, his wits – and when necessary a weapon – to earn respect.
From an early age he had been blessed with some special charisma
– true or not, his mother reported that from the age of four he had
been able to read palms and predict futures with accuracy. There
was for sure a natural sharpness about him, necessarily natural since
like most kids in Trenchtown he received an abbreviated formal
education. He took up an apprenticeship in welding (like Bunny
Livingston and the two Barrett brothers), although an accident in the
welder's yard – when fragments of hot metal lodged in one eye –
convinced Marley that music was a preferable career. Music would*

be the dominating influence from his teens onwards – his life work and his relaxation. His second love was soccer, something he picked up at school and on the streets. Marley saw it as a discipline, a way of keeping out of trouble and clearing his head. On tour with The Wailers, or relaxing at the house on Hope Road, a football would never be far away.

My father's white, my mother's black. Well, me don't dip on nobody's side, me don't dip on the black man's side nor the white man's side, me dip on God's side.

Bob Marley,
Melody Maker, 1975

49

He had leadership qualities, the kind of character that others could gravitate towards – although an element of that was thrust upon him. Within The Wailers, once Bunny Livingston and Peter Tosh had parted company with the group, he was the front man, and the principal songwriter. He provided the charismatic focus, but he was not the sole architect of the music – much of that role fell to Aston Barrett, the 'Family Man', who made sure the vehicle for Marley's stardom was a well-oiled machine.

Super-sensitive, amazingly bright, takes in a lot of things right to the back of his head. He's a natural leader, and he has some very, very heavy people around him – when I say heavy, I mean in the sense that they're very bright, very intelligent and talented . . . . It says a lot for him that they acknowledge him as their leader.

Chris Blackwell, *Melody Maker*, 1976, on Marley

I and Bob put the music together. Most times I fit a line to the instruments according to the inspiration I get from the tune when we rehearse; you know, when working out or jamming. Most times too Bob feel a ting and might just pick on him guitar and from there develop it.

Aston Barrett, *NME*, 1975

I am not a leader. Messenger. The words of the songs, not the person, is what attracts people. I don't want to be a leader, but a cheer leader.

Bob Marley, *Melody Maker*, 1977

Despite the seriousness with which he took his religion and his politics, Marley was no dour politico. Behind the inscrutability and intensity – which could equally emerge as perfectionism in the studio – lay a bubbling sense of humour, his love of football, and a joy in living.

Y'call me 'natty 'ead' . . . greeyat, because who care what you think? Me no vex meself while you laugh. Laugh and make the world laugh mon, so me dig it, so me live.

Bob Marley, *NME*, 1975, on his dreadlocks

He had a good bullshit barometer. He enjoyed winding people up. When he promoted the 'Natty Dread' album here in '75 I watched him change accents to a deeper and deeper patois, really twisting up interviewers that wouldn't understand.

Vivien Goldman, *NME*, 1981

If superstardom consists of being elusive, evasive, incoherent, unpunctual, enigmatic, all-round difficult, then Marley is no superstar.

Karl Dallas, *Melody Maker*, 1975

MoDERN iCoNS ●– BOB MARLEY

*As Marley and The Wailers found serious success,
he became a target for resentment and a magnet
for hangers-on, like any star, perhaps reinforced in
his case by the genuine poverty of his home base.*

What you must remember is that Bob's sharper
than all of us. He always used to give friends
dollars if they needed it, but now the whole world
seems to be joining in. The same guys who knew
Marley when he was in Trenchtown are talking
behind his back now, and it's sickening.
Manager **Don Taylor**, *Melody Maker*, 1976

Me love all the reggae artists, man, knowing
that they don't understand the situation and
that them can do better. Me love all of them,
cos them 'ave the same feeling as me.
Bob Marley, *NME*, 1975

We have many special musicians in this town. Let
them be delivered as individuals. Yes, there is a
lot of jealousy over Bob Marley, but everyone
realises the music must have a leader. Cassius
Clay for boxing, Bob Marley for reggae.
Prince Tony, U Roy producer, *Melody Maker*, 1976

POSITIVE VIBRATIONS

●●●

*Bob Marley's earliest contact with music was through his mother
Cedella. She was a regular churchgoer, so the young Bob – Nesta
as he was called as a child – was exposed to the music sung during
the services. He later recalled that some of his first memories
included his mother singing around the house. When she moved to
Kingston, a new musical influence entered Marley's life – the sounds
of ska were part of the Trenchtown lifestyle, and across the yards
would drift R&B captured by a neighbour's transistor radio. When
Marley struck up a friendship with Bunny Livingston, the pair of them
would sit around singing together, picking out tunes on a Heath
Robinsonesque guitar that Bunny had ingeniously constructed from a
large sardine tin, some bamboo and a cluster of wires. When they
gravitated to the free music sessions hosted by Joe Higgs at his Third
Street home, their instinctive love for music received its first
rudimentary instruction. Higgs spotted the promise in Marley's tenor
voice, and encouraged him further. Still in their mid-teens, the two
boys caught the attention of local producers like Coxsone Dodd, who
moved quickly to add them to his roster of artists. As the original
version of The Wailers came together, Marley had already added
songwriting to his vocal skills and his self-taught guitar work. Come
the end of 1963, The Wailers were recording his song 'Simmer
Down', a song written as a message both to his mother who was*

becoming increasingly concerned that Bob was falling in with the local hoodlums, and a plea to the rude boys themselves. That first single – a Number 1 hit in Jamaica – already spelt out the formula of his later songs: a lyric created out of a personal situation, delivered with real meaning, but containing a universal message and a very commercial hook line.

If God hadn'a given me a song to sing, I wouldn't have a song to sing. The song comes from God, all the time.
Bob Marley, 1976

Marley's musical skills had been learnt from other more experienced musicians in Jamaica, who recognised his fledgling talent. There was no great technical expertise – even in the mid-Seventies, when The Wailers were touring the UK, one journalist noted that of the two guitarists (Peter Tosh and Marley) and bassist Aston Barrett not one knew how to tune a guitar. It was the keyboardist who took on those duties for them. The talent was natural, heartfelt, raw, soulful.

It just happen. Natural music. Nobody show us how to play, unnerstand? I-and-I listen funky music, soul. This our soul.
Bob Marley, *Melody Maker,* 1976

There are only a few singers that could really sing the type of tunes that I really appreciate. Guys like Bob Marley could sing what I want. I say to Bob, sing that, he sing it just like I want it to sing.
Lee 'Scratch' Perry, *Black Music,* 1975

How I learn to play guitar? I teach myself. A good guitar player, him can do some real showy things, but when him a catch you watching, him a-hide it. Like a man a-hide his high cards. He don't want you to catch it so quick.

Bob Marley, 1976

On stage, Marley brought a visual dimension to the music of commitment, totally involved and completely involving. The dreadlocks he had grown from the early Seventies to conform with Rastafarian practice became a performance art in their own right, hypnotically swirling and swinging in the lights.

When the band went into 'Slave Driver', it was obvious that something very special was happening. Marley was scrubbing out those chords, and moving round the stage, his head cranking back and forth, as if clockwork driven. Every so often, he'd just stop playing guitar, and stand motionless for a split second, clutching his skull. And then he'd slash his hand across the strings again, and drive his way back into the middle of the sound.

Steve Lake, *Melody Maker*, 1973

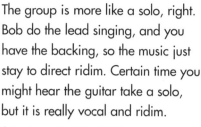

The group is more like a solo, right.
Bob do the lead singing, and you
have the backing, so the music just
stay to direct ridim. Certain time you
might hear the guitar take a solo,
but it is really vocal and ridim.

Aston Barrett, *NME*, 1975

Aston Barrett's pounding bass line kicks you
in the guts . . . Marley stands stone frozen,
singing with total concentration. Then, as
the beat steadies down and the energy
builds, Marley explodes across the stage,
dancing for a moment with dreadlocks
flying, arms stabbing the air, sorcerer's face
shining. Seconds later he's lost in a trance
again, leaving the audience gasping.

Michael Goodwin, *Rolling Stone*, 1975

Marley, he is everywhere, never still,
bending his knees sharply on the third
beat of every bar. Turning his back on
the audience and retreating to stage
rear to signify the end of a song.

Karl Dallas, *Melody Maker*, 1975

Marley's music found a new audience among the UK's punks of 1976. It was a political connection. The Clash, whose own politicisation had been triggered by watching the riots at that summer's Notting Hill Carnival, were drawn to his message of militant disaffection. Their debut album included a cover version of Junior Murvin's 'Police And Thieves', and a session with ex-Wailers producer Lee Perry ensued. Johnny Rotten was also a declared reggae fan. Marley and Perry returned the compliment by writing 'Punky Reggae Party' as the double A-side of 'Jamming' in 1977.

Listen, punk love reggae. If them were black them were Rasta, if them were white them were punk. The music – me no listen t'everything but certain t'ings me like. For instance 'God Save The Queen, fascist regime' – me like that. Ah dig the punk for that.

Bob Marley, *Melody Maker*, 1978

Black kids are being suppressed, we are being suppressed, so we've got something in common.

Paul Simonon of The Clash, 1977

When he first saw and heard about punks, for example, he thought they were pretty funny with all their coloured hair and safety pins. Were they clean? But when he started to hear about the punk ideology, his amusement turned to serious consideration and respect. He meant all that 'punky-reggae-party' stuff.

Vivien Goldman, *NME*, 1981

MUSICAL MOMENTS

• •

*The first phase of Bob Marley's musical career was as a part of
the sprawling collection of musicians working in the local
Kingston music scene. After his first two solo singles – produced
and released by Leslie Kong – The Wailers were based around
Coxsone Dodd's Studio One, backed by Dodd's army of
session men. Although they had a clear identity and a
distinctive set of harmonies – Bunny Livingston's near-falsetto,
Marley's tenor and Tosh's deeper voice – The Wailers were still
emulating the Motown and R&B sounds that were coming in
from the States. Marley would later pick out the Drifters as the
greatest influence on him in those early days, songs like 'Magic
Moment' and 'Please Stay'. It wasn't until 1966 and the
emergence of their rougher, tougher, rude boy material that The
Wailers began to acquire a specific edge. After a couple of
fallow years, during which Marley did a nine-month stint
working in the US, and both Marley and Livingston spent brief
periods in jail for possession of ganja, his career – still
intertwined completely with that of The Wailers's – took on a
new lease of life through the interest of American singer Johnny
Nash, but more importantly, thanks to the tightening up of The
Wailers's act by producer Lee Perry. Perry added the Barrett
brothers to beef up the rhythm section and created two*

collectable albums, 'Soul Rebels' and 'Soul Revolution'. With Marley's increasing belief in Rastafarianism, the basic patterns were in place for The Wailers's first Island album, refined and developed through successive releases, and finding their perfect moment in the 'Live!' album that captured the Marley-Wailers-audience mutual appreciation society in full cry. Thereafter, according to most critics, the musical ideas were reworked and formularised, however special individual moments or songs might be.

Some music can't go in a class or a bracket. Music free and without prejudice. Music don't care . . . music just wanta be.
Bob Marley, 1975

After The Wailers signed with Island, they returned to Kingston to lay down the tracks for their first release, 'Catch A Fire', at Harry Johnson's studio on Roosevelt Avenue. They brought the tapes of those sessions back to London, where the sound was sweetened with input from keyboard player John 'Rabbit' Bundrick and Wayne Perkins (the Muscle Shoals's session guitarist who was a frontrunner for the Stones's guitar slot when Mick Taylor left). With its distinctive Zippo lighter sleeve design, the whole package had been given an extra dimension of marketability.

Everything one needs to know about Bob Marley's conquest of Rock Babylon is really there in that first astonishing song on 'Catch A Fire'. The opening seconds could almost be a snatch from some Grateful Dead jam. A clavinet gurgles into life over a heartbeat of a kick drum and ushers it towards the first verse. From the platform of the organ and the chicken-scratch bounce of the guitars emerges the raw, proud voice of the lead Wailer, lifted aloft by the lamenting tones of Peter Tosh and Bunny Livingston. The whole sound has a cohesion new to reggae, with the mix perfectly tailored to white ears.

Barney Hoskyns, *Mojo*, 1995

This is the music of the people. Genuine ghetto music and not the tarted-up pastiche of get-rich-quick record companies out for a killing . . . . Definitely one of the best records of the year.

Roy Carr, *NME*, 1973

He's an accomplished and intelligent lyricist, retaining the simple groove that's so attractive while getting across in a clear direct way ideas that have previously been considered too 'sophisticated' for mere pop music.

Martin Hayman, *Sounds*, 1973

'Catch A Fire' was an introduction. It was for people get in and listen.

Bob Marley, 1974

67

By the third album 'Natty Dread' (from the Rasta hairstyle 'knotty dreads') Tosh and Wailer had parted company as Marley was brought increasingly into the foreground. Horns, harmonica and the I-Threes rounded out the sound, and the album started to earn serious attention; for many critics this was the seminal Marley release.

It confirms Bob Marley's place among the canon of truly innovative and challenging voices in black music. It is, perhaps, the closest we're going to get to the Free-wheelin' Bob Dylan.

Neil Spencer, *NME*, 1975

This album achieves a good balance between the traditionally earthy Wailers' music and the influences of pop/rock music. It is aggressive, sober and serious. Often it is a threatening and lyrical force of harmony, melody and rhythm.

Carl Gayle, *Black Music*, 1974

Predictably, 'Natty Dread' itself was the hit of the night, and whenever Marley shook his hair he got a round of applause. It's been a very long time since anyone's seen an audience applaud an artist's hair, but then it's been a very long time since hair has *represented* anything specific to any part of the subculture.

Charles Shaar Murray, *NME*, 1975, on the Wailers at the Lyceum, London

This is where the legend truly began. Two nights at London's Lyceum on 18 and 19 July 1975 and the word was out. The band were kicking, Marley was connecting with an audience who understood. Some quick thinking by Island and the moment was captured for posterity's pleasure.

The first night at the Lyceum, the intensity and the vibe were just nuts. They opened up the roof because it was so hot. Chris asked if I wanted to record the following night's show. I said, Get the Rolling Stones' Mobile and I'll do it. The recording would never have been as good if it hadn't been for Dave Harper, who mixed the live sound out front. So much of the mix is to do with those live hall mikes, and you can hear that in 'No Woman, No Cry', the ultimate singalong.

Steve Smith, co-producer of 'Live!', *Mojo*, 1995

Suffice it that this is everything that a Wailers 'live' album should be – an irresistible sweat-drenched 'live' classic. Throughout the band plays exemplary, brilliant stuff grooving with sultry power and pulsing with rhythms that pervade every aspect of their playing.

Neil Spencer, *NME*, 1975

THE LION SLEEPS

By the November of 1980, rumours about Marley's state of health were circulating throughout the music press – there was talk of tumours, of cancer, following his collapse during an American tour that Autumn. The record company and Rita continued to deny it, a taped message from Marley was released to reassure everybody. The truth was that those closest to Marley were trying to protect him. He was extremely ill. At the end of the year he entered the clinic of the unorthodox cancer specialist Dr Josef Issels, at Lake Tegern in Bavaria. But after five months there – during which he had had to endure the spiritual pain of shaving off his dreadlocks – there was no more help that Issels could provide for Marley; he was flown to Florida (where his mother was living) and died there four days later. A Cedars Of Lebanon hospital spokesman had said that by that point there was nothing they could do for him except to ease the pain and keep him comfortable. His last words to Cedella were 'Mother, don't cry. I'll be alright'.

Bob Marley's death was honoured in Jamaica by a period of national mourning – memorial concerts and tributes marked his passing. But Marley had died intestate, and sadly, the next ten years were taken up with legal wrangling about who owned the rights to his estate, disputes settled only in 1991 by a Supreme Court decision to award ownership to a consortium consisting of Marley's family and one of Chris Blackwell's companies. Now the lion could be allowed to sleep in peace.

Me not of the world, y'know. Me live in the world but I'm not of the world.
Bob Marley, 1975

Marley's loss was felt immediately. He had become a figurehead for his race, for his religion, for his music. Now his status would continue to grow: the posthumous compilation album 'Legend', released in 1984, was an immediate success and then sold on and on. 1992's 'Songs Of Freedom' further detailed his musical legacy, and in 1994 Marley was the first Third World musician to be inducted into the Rock And Roll Hall Of Fame. Sadly, reggae – to which he had contributed so much – began to run out of steam.

If the collapse of punk took reggae's crutch away, then Bob Marley's death cut off its legs. He had subtly taken militant reggae into the mainstream and was keeping it there. With him gone, reggae lost a lot of credibility.
Drummie of Aswad, Q magazine, 1987

I can say nothing other than that it's a terrible, awful loss. Bob's career was always much larger than music – and there was much more to come.
Chris Blackwell, 1981

Without such a massive figurehead, reggae musicians had no one to aspire to and started looking in other directions.
David Hinds of Steel Pulse, Q magazine, 1987

After Marley's death, his son Ziggy Marley carried on the family tradition, and achieved some success with his group the Melody Makers, formed with three of his sisters and brothers. The surviving Wailers occasionally regrouped for special occasions and the I-Threes briefly reconvened, but the music inevitably lacked one vital ingredient – the man himself.

A man of lively intelligence, insatiable curiosity, profuse humour, and unwavering faith and commitment, he was also endowed in great measure with the musical and performing talents to conquer the hearts of millions to whom his Rastafarian beliefs were indecipherable at best and plainly offensive at worst.

Neil Spencer, *NME*, 1981

Me name David but me big Bowie fan. So at the time of the 'Ziggy Stardust' album, me call meself Ziggy and now everyone do.

Ziggy, *Melody Maker*, 1988

My music will go on forever. Maybe it's a fool say that, but when me know facts me can say facts. My music go on forever.

Bob Marley, 1975

While the world mourned the death of a figurehead, Marley's last words to his mother were the inspiration for her own tribute to Bob, a song called 'Mother Don't Cry'. Marley is gone, but the legend lives on in his music.

The greatest thing them can say is about death – 'cos them say you die and go to 'eaven after all this sufferation. To go through all sufferation for that! 'S like after me sick, me go to the doctor. No, the greatest thing is *life*, mon, life.
Bob Marley, *NME*, 1975

I don't believe in death, neither in flesh nor in spirit. You have to AVOID IT. Some people don't figure it's such a great thing. They don't know how long they can preserve it. Preservation is the gift of God, the gift of God is life, the wages of sin is Death. When a man does wickedness he's gone up there and dead.
Bob Marley, *NME*, 1979

I don't see reggae music as like the twist, I see reggae music as music. As far as me is concerned, I never give it a name – just play music.
Bob Marley, *Melody Maker*, 1975

THE MUSIC

★★★★★   **Essential listening**
★★★   **OK**
★   **Frankly, not the best!**

SINGLES

THE WAILERS

Pre-Island Records releases
available on compilations include

Simmer Down/I Don't Need Your Love – 1965 ★★★

Rude Boy/B-side by Rolando Al and the Soul Brothers – 1966 ★★★

Duppy Conqueror/Justice – 1970 ★★★½

Small Axe/All In One – February 1971 ★★★★

Trenchtown Rock/Grooving Kingdom – November 1971 ★★★½

BOB MARLEY & THE WAILERS

Concrete Jungle/No More Trouble – July 1973 ★★★

No Woman, No Cry (live)/Kinky Reggae – August 1975,
               reissued June 1981 b/w Jamming ★★★★★

Exodus/Exodus (Dub) – June 1977 ★★★★½

Jamming/Punky Reggae Party – December 1977 ★★★★

Is This Love/Crisis – February 1978 ★★★★

Satisfy My Soul/Smile Jamaica – May 1978 ★★★

Could You Be Loved/One Drop – May 1980 ★★★★

Three Little Birds/Every Need Got An Ego To Feed – August 1980 ★★★½

No Woman, No Cry (live)/Jamming – June 1981 ★★★★

Buffalo Soldier/Buffalo (Dub) – April 1983 ★★★★

One Love/People Get Ready – April 1984 ★★★★½

Iron Zion Lion/Could You Be Loved – September 1992 ★★★½

ALBUMS

THE WAILERS

Catch A Fire – April 1973 ★★★★½
Concrete Jungle/Slave Driver/400 Years/Stop That Train/Rock It Baby /Stir It Up/Kinky Reggae/No More Trouble/Midnight Ravers
'Catch A Fire' is beautiful, reassuringly mellow, full-sounding music. Try it. Try listening to a track like 'Stop That Train' or 'Stir It Up' and try to forget about the damn song, try to get it out of your mind. It just won't leave you in peace.
Phonograph Record Magazine, 1973

Burnin' – November 1973 ★★★★½
Get Up, Stand Up/Hallelujah Time/I Shot The Sheriff/Burnin' And Lootin'/Put It On/Small Axe/Pass It On/Duppy Conqueror/One Foundation/Rastaman Chant
'Burnin'' marked a widening of Marley's audience through Eric Clapton's hit version of 'I Shot The Sheriff' and brought the group mainstream pop stardom. The addition of Earl Lindo to the group on this album heralded a return to their musical roots, free from outside commercial interference.

BOB MARLEY & THE WAILERS

Natty Dread – October 1974 ★★★★★
Lively Up Yourself/No Woman, No Cry/Them Belly Full (But We Hungry)/Rebel Music (3 O'Clock Road Block)/So Jah Seh/Natty Dread/Bend Down Low/Talkin' Blues'/Revolution
'Natty Dread' is exquisite. It does for reggae what Marvin Gaye's 'Let's Get It On' did for soul – spreads it right out, lays it right back and turns it around and around on itself.
Idris Walters, *Let It Rock,* 1975

Live! – November 1975 ★★★
Trenchtown Rock/Burnin' & Lootin'/Them Belly Full /Lively Up Yourself/No Woman, No Cry/I Shot The Sheriff/Get Up, Stand Up
While 'Live!' may not be as good as the set I saw at the 30,000 seat National Stadium in Kingston it's a toss-up whether this record or 'Natty Dread' is better. The audience response is electrifying and both the Wailers and the I-Threes vocalists are in top form. One of the best live albums ever.
Ed Ward, *Rolling Stone,* 1976

Rastaman Vibrations
– April 1976 ★★★★¹⁄₂
Positive Vibration/Rock Roots
Reggae/Johnny Was (Woman
Hang Her Head And Cry)/Cry
To Me/Want More/Crazy
Baldhead/Who The Cap Fit/Night
Shift/War/Rat Race
*A good album certainly, perhaps
even a great one . . . .*
Neil Spencer, *NME, 1976*

'Rastaman Vibrations' stayed in the
US charts for 22 weeks, where it
peaked at Number 8; it reached
Number 15 in the UK. 'War' has
been hailed as one of the greatest
Rastafarian songs – the lyrics
are based on one of Haile
Selassie's speeches.

Exodus – May 1977 ★★★★
Natural Mystic/So Much Things To
Say/Guiltiness/The Heathen/Exodus/Jamming/Waiting In Vain/Turn Your Lights
Down Low/Three Little Birds/One Love – People Get Ready
*'Exodus' arrives with felicitous timing: it's the first great summer album of 1977.
'Exodus' seems almost like a reward for making it through winter.*
Charles Shaar Murray, *NME, 1977*

Kaya – March 1978 ★★¹⁄₂
Easy Skanking/Kaya/Is This Love/The Sun Is Shining/Satisfy My Soul/She's
Gone/Misty Morning/Crisis/Running Away/Time Will Tell
*Marley is never going to make a BAD record, and this may well serve as a natural
follow-up to 'Exodus'.*
Ray Coleman, *Melody Maker, 1978*

Babylon By Bus – December 1978 ★★★
Positive Vibration/Punky Reggae Party/Exodus/Stir It Up/Rat Race/Concrete
Jungle/Kinky Reggae/Lively Up Yourself/Rebel Music (3 O'Clock Road

Block)/War – No More Trouble/Is This Love/The Heathen/Jamming
This live double album was recorded at the Pavilion in Paris, while Bob and the Wailers were on a world tour. It reached Number 40 in the UK, but only Number 102 in the US.

Survival – October 1979 ★★★
So Much Trouble In The World/Zimbabwe/Top Rankin'/Babylon System/Survival/Africa Unite/One Drop/Ride Natty Ride/Ambush In The Night/Wake Up And Live
Some people mellow as they get older. Bob Marley gets angrier and wiser. Following the relaxed, self-fulfilled 'Exodus' and 'Kaya,' 'Survival' marks a surprising but welcome return to the frontline of political entertainment with a passion strengthened by reasoned analysis and the most beautiful singing I've heard in a long time.
Chris Bohn, *Melody Maker*, 1979

Uprising – June 1980 ★★★¹/₂
Coming In From The Cold/Real Situation/Bad Card/We And Them/Work/ Zion Train/Pimper's Paradise/Could You Be Loved/Forever Loving Jah/ Redemption Song
One song, a slender acoustic piece called 'Redemption Song', puts the seal on 'Uprising' as a Marley album of great worth. The Wailers play as if they think and breathe with one mind and body creating a seamless flow of music bursting with melodic sensitivity and percussive life.
John Orme, *Melody Maker*, 1980

Legend – May 1984 ★★★★★
Is This Love/No Woman, No Cry/Could You Be Loved/Three Little Birds/Buffalo Soldier/Get Up, Stand Up/Stir It Up/One Love – People Get Ready/I Shot The Sheriff/Waiting In Vain/Redemption Song/Satisfy My Soul/Exodus/Jamming
Bob Marley was one of the greats, and it is a joy to encounter the passions of the songs on this greatest hits package. 'Legend' is an excellent way to meet up with some music that's too good to pass by.
Christopher Connelly, *Rolling Stone*, 1984

THE HISTORY

Key Dates

6 February 1945
Robert Nesta Marley is born at Nine Miles, St Ann's,
Jamaica. Son of Norval Sinclair Marley, a fifty-
something Liverpool-born captain in the British Army,
and the teenage Cedella Booker. This birthdate is
believed to be correct although no birth certificate
has ever been found.

December 1962
Marley, having left school at 14, and trained as a
welder, is concentrating on music. He records two singles, 'Judge Not (Unless You
Judge Yourself)' and 'One Cup Of Coffee' at a local studio run by Leslie Kong,
owner of the Beverley's label.

1963
Forms the Wailing Rudeboys (later becoming The Wailin' Wailers) with Trenchtown
pals Peter Tosh and Bunny Livingston; they are joined by Junior Braithwaite and
female vocalists Beverley Kelso and Cherry Green. The group undergoes extensive
tuition with vocalist Joe Higgs and drummer Alvin 'Secco' Patterson, and records
some 70-80 tracks for the Studio One label with Coxsone Dodd.

January 1964
The Wailers's first single, 'Simmer Down', reaches Number 1 in Jamaica's JBC
Radio chart. The group begin to release a series of singles that feature regularly in
the Jamaican charts.

February 1966
Marries Rita (Alpharita) Anderson. The next day he leaves his new bride and their
first child to head to Wilmington, Delaware, USA, where he joins his mother.

November 1966
Marley returns to Jamaica with some savings, setting up a record store in Kingston
with Rita. Rita has converted to Rastafarianism, changing her name to Ganette
Mander (meaning 'Paradise'), following the visit to Jamaica of Haile Selassie I,
Emperor of Ethiopia.

1967
Reunites with Peter Tosh and Bunny Livingston, releasing singles on the Beverley's label. They cut a local hit, 'Bend Down Low', at Studio One and create their own label, Wail'M'Soul'M – but the venture is a commercial failure. Marley hooks up with American artist Johnny Nash (who in 1972 storms the UK charts with Marley's 1968 composition 'Stir It Up') and Danny Sims, Nash's manager, signs Marley to Nash's JAD label.

November 1968
Marley has begun exploring Rastafarianism. Meets Mortimo Planno of the Divine Theocratic Temple of Rastafari in Kingston. Beginning of Rastafarian influence on Marley's music. Bob, Bunny, Peter and Rita record on Johnny Nash's JAD label, produced by Arthur Jenkins.

1969
Along with the rest of the Wailers, Marley fully embraces Rastafarianism. They link up with top local producer Lee 'Scratch' Perry on their newly formed Tuff Gong label. Perry brings in the Barrett brothers, Aston and Carlton, as the Wailers's rhythm section: they will become an integral part of the group's sound.

1970
Debut Wailers album 'Soul Rebel' released.

1972
After a difficult, though creative period, The Wailers, finding themselves alone in London and effectively left to their own devices by Johnny Nash and Danny Sims, sign with Island Records's boss Chris Blackwell.

April 1973
Their debut release on Island is 'Catch A Fire' – heavily promoted by the label. A UK tour, including key dates at the Speakeasy in London, attracts rock critics and other Island stars – the band's UK profile is further raised by appearances on BBC Radio One and BBC TV's Old Grey Whistle Test.

July 1973
The Wailers appear at Max's Kansas City Club in New York (the centre of American new wave activity a year or so later), supporting Bruce Springsteen.

November 1973
Second Island album 'Burnin'' released.

MoDERN iCoNS – BOB MARLEY

August 1974
Eric Clapton reaches Number 1 in the US singles charts with his cover version of Marley's 'I Shot The Sheriff', taken from Clapton's '461 Ocean Boulevard'.

October 1974
'Natty Dread' released. A significant difference on this album is that the group is now called Bob Marley and The Wailers. Tosh and Livingston have gone solo, possibly upset that Marley is now being heavily promoted as the frontman. Marley adds The I-Threes (female singers wife Rita, Judy Mowatt and Marcia Griffiths). Additional musicians on the album include Al Anderson (guitar) and Bernard 'Touter' Harvey (keyboards).

July 1975
The new Wailers play two classic dates at the Lyceum London, immortalised later that year on the album 'Live!' from which a live version of 'No Woman, No Cry' is also released. The band has been enhanced by Junior Marvin (guitar), Tyrone Downie (keyboards, replacing Harvey) and Alvin 'Secco' Patterson on percussion, Marley's original rhythm tutor from the early Sixties.

May 1976
The Wailers play the Roxy, Los Angeles – a concert later listed in *Rolling Stone's* 1987 feature *Live! Twenty concerts that changed rock'n'roll*. 'Rastaman Vibrations' released.

June 1976
Bob Marley And The Wailers headline a festival in Wales – 20,000 people are expected, but because of heavy rain only 2,000 turn up. Most shelter inside terraces so the group ends up playing to only around 100 people in the field.

December 1976
Gunmen break into Marley's home in Kingston during the Jamaican general election campaign. Present are Marley, Rita, their manager Don Taylor, other friends and five children. All the adults are shot and wounded – Marley is shot in his upper body and arm, Rita receives a head wound, friend Lewis Griffith is seriously wounded as is Don Taylor, but all survive. Marley hides out in Jamaica's Blue Mountains after release from hospital. Four days later he performs at the 'Smile Jamaica' festival, although he is unable to play guitar due to his wounds. Rita sings, with her head in bandages. The couple then take a break of eighteen months away from Jamaica.

Spring 1977
The Wailers are based in London, on and off, for three months while working on their next album, during which time Marley and Aston Barrett are arrested and fined for possession of 'erb.

June 1977
'Exodus' is released – it reaches Number 8 in the UK album charts, later hitting Number 20 in the States.

September 1977
In Miami, a cancerous growth is diagnosed on one of Marley's toes – the press is informed that it is a foot injury received while playing soccer.

Feb 1978
The album 'Kaya' is recorded in England: the single 'Is This Love' reaches the UK Top Ten.

April 1978
Bob Marley And The Wailers play the One Love Peace concert at Kingston's National Arena – an attempt to link Jamaica's feuding political parties; Marley symbolically joins the hands of bitter rivals Michael Manley and Edward Seaga.

December 1978
Marley makes first, short trip to Rastafarianism's spiritual homeland Ethiopia. The second Wailers live album 'Babylon By Bus' is released.

February 1979
The Wailers are the first reggae act to play at Harlem's famous Apollo Theater, in front of a backdrop featuring an Ethiopian flag, a portrait of Haile Selassie, and a collage of Marcus Garvey and other black freedom fighters.

April 1980
Marley performs at Zimbabwe's Independence Day celebrations, before undertaking a major European tour, which includes a headlining appearance at the 'Summer Garden Party' at the Crystal Palace Bowl.

July 1980
The single 'Could You Be Loved', taken from the album 'Uprising', reaches UK Number 5.

September 1980
During dates at Madison Square Garden, New York, supporting the Commodores, Marley collapses while jogging. Cancer is detected.

November 1980
Marley is baptised at Kingston's Ethiopian Orthodox Church, marking his conversion to Christian Rastafarianism: he takes the name Berhane Selassie. The following month he flies to the Bavarian clinic of Dr Josef Issels. Stevie Wonder has a Top 5 US hit with 'Master Blaster (Jammin')', his Marley tribute.

11 May 1981
Marley dies at Miami's Cedars of Lebanon Hospital, days after arriving. He is buried on 21 May after lying in state at the National Arena, Kingston.

July 1981
A re-release of 'No Woman, No Cry' charts in the UK.

August 1981
A tribute to Marley in Montego Bay, Jamaica, forms part of the Fourth International Reggae Sunsplash Festival, including an appearance by the Melody Makers – four of Marley's children.

May 1984
The 'Legend' compilation is released: it spends 12 weeks in total at Number 1 in the UK album charts, and also becomes a permanent fixture in the US album charts.

May 1986
The Marley Museum opens in Kingston on the site of his home, headquarters of Tuff Gong Records.

1990
Marley's mother Cedella records and releases a tribute to her son – backed by The Wailers on a gospel/reggae set called 'Awake Zion'.

February 1990
6 February is declared a national holiday in Jamaica.

December 1991
After more than ten years of legal wrangles caused by Marley dying without making a will, the Jamaican Supreme Court makes the decision that Marley's assets should be sold to his family who is given control in tandem with Chris Blackwell's Island Logic.

January 1994
Posthumous induction of Bob Marley to the Rock And Roll Hall of Fame. The induction speech is given by U2 singer Bono.

THE CAST

Aston 'Family Man' Barrett. Born 22 November 1946, Rollington, East Kingston. A welding apprentice, he learns guitar and forms the Hippy Boys in 1967 working for various producers, including Lee 'Scratch' Perry. Barrett is part of Perry's band Upsetters who tour following the 1969 UK chart success of 'Return Of Django'. Through Perry, he is involved with The Wailers before joining permanently. His rhythms are used by Johnny Nash on Nash's first major reggae album 'I Can See Clearly Now', and with brother Carlton he backs artists including John Holt, Errol Dunkley, Keith Hudson, Gregory Isaacs and the Maytals. His first major impact – his stylistic signature is the placing of spaces between bass riffs – comes on the 'Catch A Fire' album.

Carlton Barrett. Born 17 December 1950, Kingston. Like elder brother Aston he is part of Lee Perry's Upsetters and then The Wailers. Together they form the backbone of The Wailers's sound. Carlton is shot dead on 17 April 1987 outside his Kingston home by an unknown assailant.

Chris Blackwell. Born 22 June 1937 into a well-off white Jamaican family, Blackwell attends Harrow School in England before returning to Jamaica. He forms Island Records in 1962: many Jamaican artists appear on Island and its subsidiary labels, which include Black Swan and Sue (latter reportedly the model for the Beatles's Apple Records; George Harrison says it should be 'small and funky' like Sue). Bob Marley's first singles from 1962 are distributed by Island. Jamaican singer Millie's 1964 'My Boy Lollipop' is a hit single, but there is no breakthrough reggae artist, so in the late Sixties the company changes direction to English rock, with the likes of Traffic, Free, Fairport Convention, Nick Drake and Jethro Tull. The Jamaican link is maintained by the specially formed Trojan label, with Jimmy Cliff the main artist. Signs The Wailers in 1972, and finally achieves his dream of a major international reggae artist. With the Marley family he acquires Bob Marley's estate in 1991.

MoDERN iCoNS – BOB MARLEY

Coxsone Dodd. Born Clement Seymour Dodd, he is nicknamed Sir Coxsone after a famous cricketer who plays for Yorkshire. Sets up one of the first sound systems in Jamaica, in competition with Earl Reid and others, leading to famous sound system 'clashes' in the Fifties. Begins producing own music (although not a musician, he has impeccable musical judgment) as Jamaican R&B develops into ska. His Studio One is a hugely influential training ground for many major Jamaican musicians and producers, including Prince Buster, Lee 'Scratch' Perry, Winston Holness, the Maytals and The Wailers. Eventually the studio closes, and Dodd moves to New York in the mid-Eighties, celebrating 35 years in the business with two major shows in 1991.

The I-Threes. Marcia Griffiths: born 1954, Kingston. Possibly the most consistently successful female vocalist to emerge from reggae. She is contracted by Coxsone Dodd and has a Jamaican Number 1 in 1968 with 'Feel Like A Teenager' and a UK hit, 'Young Gifted And Black', with Bob Andy in 1970. Solo career highlights include the 1989 hit 'Electric Boogie' recorded with the surviving Wailers. **Rita Marley**, born Alpharita Constantia Anderson, is a member of the Soulettes group based at Coxsone Dodd's Studio One, where she meets Bob Marley – they marry in 1966. She enjoys a solo career before and after Marley's death. Her 1980's poignant album 'Who Feels It Knows It' is recorded during Marley's final illness. Her subsequent solo career includes the 1991 album 'We Must Carry On'. **Judy Mowatt**: born 1952, Kingston. Sings with the female vocal trio the Gaylets (also known as the Gaytones) in the mid-Sixties. She goes solo in 1970, and sets up her own label Ashandan in 1975. She releases a self-produced album on Tuff Gong called 'Black Woman' in 1979 and continues her solo career thereafter.

Leslie Kong. Born 1933 Kingston. A Chinese Jamaican, he runs an ice cream parlour cum record store called Beverley's. He moves into record production with Jimmy Cliff, Bob Marley (who cuts his two debut singles with Kong), Desmond Dekker, and the Maytals. He has a major hit with Desmond Dekker with 1967's '007' and 1969's 'Israelites'; also cracks the UK charts with the Melodians's 'Rivers Of Babylon'. Repackages some Wailers recordings as 'The Best Of The Wailers' in 1971; the compilation sells well, but within weeks a heart attack kills him.

Bunny 'Wailer' Livingston. Born Neville O'Riley Livingston 10 April 1947, Kingston. Lives under same roof as Bob Marley in Trenchtown – he and Marley have a half-sister in common. His high tenor voice is a vital ingredient in The Wailers's harmony sound and he contributes songs including 'Hallelujah Time' and 'Pass It On'. Leaves the Wailers in 1974 and sets up Solomonic label; first solo album, 'Blackheart Man', is released in 1976, the title track is deemed to be a masterpiece. Continues to release solo albums including 'Tribute To The Late Hon. Robert Nesta Marley, O.M.' in 1981.

Ziggy Marley. Born David Marley 17 October 1968 – Ziggy is his own choice of name (he's a big Bowie fan). Forms the Melody Makers (including siblings Cedella, Stephen and Sharon) in 1979, signing to EMI USA and releasing albums including 'Play The Game Right' and 'Hey World!'. They subsequently sign to Virgin in 1988 with producers Tina Weymouth and Chris Frantz of Talking Heads: the album 'Conscious Party' is followed by 'One Bright Day'. His daughter, born the day of the Jamaican Supreme Court decision over Marley's estate, is named Justice.

Other Wailers. Of the original members, **Junior Braithwaite** leaves to move to Chicago in 1962, **Cherry Green** can't hack it and is fired at around the same time, and **Beverley Kelso** loses interest while Marley is in the States in 1966. After Tosh and Livingston leave The Wailers, regular members include American blues rock guitarist **Al Anderson** (from Montclair, New Jersey) who has been working at Island Studios with ex-Traffic member Chris Wood and has previously played with John Martyn; organist **Bernard 'Touter' Harvey**; guitarists **Earl Smith**, **Junior Marvin** and **Donald Kinsey** (another American); and keyboardists **Tyrone Downie** and **Earl 'Wire' Lindo**.

Lee 'Scratch' Perry, also known as 'The Upsetter'. Born Rainford Hugh, 28 March 1936, Hanover, Jamaica. One of the best known Jamaican producer/engineers among rock audiences: his Junior Murvin track 'Police And Thieves' is acclaimed among UK punks, The Clash recording a cover version, and inviting Perry to produce their own 'Complete Control'. Perry starts out working with Coxsone Dodd's sound system in the Fifties, during which time he writes a tune for a new dance called the Chicken Scratch, hence his nickname. Works with Coxsone in late Fifties and early Sixties auditioning potential artists, records as a vocalist in his own right, and from 1963 is producing his own releases. After falling out with Coxsone in 1966 (he

writes a scathing track called 'The Upsetter' about Dodd, which gives him his other nickname), he continues on his own. Creates band called the Upsetters whose 'Return Of Django' is a Top 5 hit in the UK in 1969. A touring version of the band includes Aston and Carlton Barrett. Then produces The Wailers through to 1971 (a period some critics consider The Wailers's best work), and continues to work with Marley on tracks including 'Jah Live' and 'Punky Reggae Party', as well as working with U-Roy and Dillinger. In 1974 he sets up his own studio Black Ark. After the studio is destroyed in 1980, he relocates to Britain, continuing to release solo albums outside the mainstream.

Don Taylor. He meets Marley when The Wailers support Marvin Gaye at a Kingston show in 1974. Taylor, a Jamaican who has relocated to America, has been involved in management for various R&B artists and is now part of the Gaye tour personnel. Persuades Marley to let him mange the band. Critically injured in the 1976 attempt on Marley's life, but survives. Falls out with Marley in 1980 after allegations that Taylor skimmed money from concert advance: Marley writes 'Bad Card' as an attack on Taylor for the 'Uprising' album.

Peter Tosh. Born Winston Hubert McIntosh 19 October 1944, Church Lincoln, Westmoreland, Jamaica. Meets Marley and Bunny Livingston as teenagers in Trenchtown at Joe Higgs's music sessions. Tall, tough, a karate expert, Tosh writes singles in the early days and some of the best known Wailers tracks, including 'Get Up, Stand Up'. Leaves the Wailers in 1974 when Marley is moved into prominence, and sets up label Diplo Him. His ganja law reform album 'Legalize it' is released in 1976 (he falls out with Marley over the latter's refusal to loan money for it) and has an international hit in 1977 with 'Equal Rights'. After signing to the Stones's label in 1978 he releases three albums, the first 'Bush Doctor' appearing in 1978, and his band, including Sly and Robbie, backs the Stones on tour. A political dissenter in Jamaica, he endures several beatings. Leaves the Stones's label in 1981, moves to EMI and releases 'Mama Africa' in 1983. On 11 September 1987 he is shot dead in a possibly drugs-related incident at his house, five months after Carlton Barrett is shot. In 1988 he posthumously wins a Grammy for best reggae album for 1987's 'No Nuclear War'.

THE BOOKS

Bob Marley: Conquering Lion Of Reggae – Stephen Davis (Plexus) 1994
Bob Marley In His Own Words – Ian McCann (Omnibus) 1993
Bob Marley: An Intimate Portrait By His Mother – Cedella Booker
      with Anthony Winkler (Viking) 1996
Bob Marley: Reggae King Of The World – Malika Whitney &
      Dermott Hussey (Kingston Publishers) 1984
Bob Marley: Spirit Dancer – Bruce W. Talamon (Norton) 1994
Catch A Fire: The Life Of Bob Marley – Timothy White (Omnibus) 1983
Complete Guide To The Music Of Bob Marley – Ian McCann (Omnibus) 1994
So Much Things To Say: My Life As Bob Marley's Manager – Don Taylor
      (Blake) 1995

PICTURE CREDITS

Pages 2-3 LFI. **Page 5** Paul Cox/LFI. **Page 8** Ebet Roberts/Redferns. **Page 11** LFI. **Page 12** Glenn A. Baker Archives/Redferns. **Page 13** Jill Furmanowsky/LFI. **Page 14** LFI. **Page 15** Ebet Roberts/Redferns. **Page 16** LFI. **Page 19** Jill Furmanowsky/LFI. **Page 20** Michael Ochs Archives/Redferns. **Page 21** LFI. **Page 23** Ebet Roberts/Redferns. **Page 25** (t) Ian Dickson/Redferns; (bl) LFI; (br) David Redfern/Redferns. **Page 26** (t) Ebet Roberts/Redferns; (b) Michael Putland/LFI. **Page 29** (t) Ebet Roberts/Redferns; (b) David Redfern/Redferns. **Page 30** Glenn A. Baker Archives/Redferns. **Page 31** Glenn A. Baker Archives/Redferns. **Page 33** (t) Andrew Putler/Redferns; (b) Michael Ochs Archives/Redferns. **Page 35** LFI. **Page 36** Michael Ochs Archives/Redferns. **Page 38** (t) Gai Terrell/Redferns; (b) Gai Terrell/Redferns. **Page 39** Gai Terrell/Redferns. **Page 41** (l) Pennie Smith/LFI; (r) Kevin Cummins/LFI. **Pages 42-3** Jill Furmanowsky/LFI. **Pages 44-5** (t) Ian Dickson/Redferns; (b) Mike Prior/Redferns. **Pages 46-7** Mike Prior/Redferns. **Page 49** (t) LFI; (b) LFI. **Page 51** (t) Ian Dickson/Redferns; (b) Paul Cox/LFI. **Pages 52-3** Ebet Roberts/Redferns. **Pages 54-5** Graham Wiltshire/Redferns. **Page 57** (t) Jill Furmanowsky/LFI; (b) Mike Prior/Redferns. **Pages 58-9** Mike Prior/Redferns. **Page 59** LFI. **Page 60** (t) LFI; (b) Kevin Cummins/LFI. **Page 61** (t) Kevin Cummins/LFI; (b) LFI. **Page 63** (t) Kevin Cummins/LFI; (b) David Redfern/Redferns. **Pages 64-5** Ebet Roberts/Redferns. **Page 67** (l) Paul Cox/LFI; (r) Courtesy of Island Records. **Page 69** (l) Courtesy of Island Records; (tr) LFI; (mr) Jill Furmanowsky/LFI; (br) Mike Prior/Redferns. **Page 70** David Redfern/Redferns. **Page 71** (l) Mike Prior/Redferns; (r) Courtesy of Island Records. **Page 72** Ebet Roberts/Redferns. **Page 73** Ebet Roberts/Redferns. **Page 74** LFI. **Pages 76-7** Jill Furmanowsky/LFI. **Page 78** (t) LFI; (b) Erica Echenberg/Redferns. **Page 80** Ian Dickson/Redferns. **Page 82** Jill Furmanowsky/LFI. **Page 83** Jill Furmanowsky/LFI. **Page 84** Michael Ochs Archives/Redferns. **Page 87** Mike Prior/Redferns. **Page 89** Ian Dickson/Redferns. **Page 90** Gai Terrell/Redferns. **Page 93** LFI. **Pages 94-5** LFI.

Every effort has been made to contact copyright holders.
If any omissions do occur the publisher would be
delighted to give full credit in subsequent reprints and editions.